WOODROW
WILSON

PRESIDENTIAL ✦ LEADERS

WOODROW WILSON

CAROL DOMMERMUTH-COSTA

⌐ LERNER PUBLICATIONS COMPANY / MINNEAPOLIS

To Aunt Helen
Always my favorite aunt—

Lerner Publications Company
A division of Lerner Publishing Group
241 First Avenue North
Minneapolis, MN 55401 U.S.A.

Website address: www.lernerbooks.com

Library of Congress Cataloging-in-Publication Data

Dommermuth-Costa, Carol.
    Woodrow Wilson / by Carol Dommermuth-Costa.
        p.   cm. — (Presidential leaders)
    Summary: Profiles the United States president who grew up during the Civil War and brought the nation into the first World War, yet was called the "president of peace."
    Includes bibliographical references and index.
    ISBN: 0–8225–0094–9 (lib. bdg. : alk. paper)
    1. Wilson, Woodrow, 1856–1924—Juvenile literature. 2. Presidents—United States—Biography—Juvenile literature. [1. Wilson, Woodrow, 1856–1924. 2. Presidents.] I. Title. II. Series.
E767 .D66   2003
973.91'3'092—dc21   2002000449

Manufactured in the United States of America
1 2 3 4 5 6 – JR – 08 07 06 05 04 03

CONTENTS

◇

*Wilson had tough decisions to make
as president of the United States.*

INTRODUCTION

A DIRE DECISION

"It is clear that nations must in the future be governed by the same high code of honor that we demand of individuals."
Woodrow Wilson

A soft spring rain fell in Washington, D.C., as the president's motorcade drove up the hill to the Capitol. Soldiers stood at attention along the streets. Thousands cheered and waved flags. The date was April 2, 1917, and the president of the United States had called a special session of Congress.

The hall was deathly silent as President Woodrow Wilson stepped into the room. All eyes were on him, and every face wore a somber, expectant expression. This meeting was an unusual one. The president had made a very difficult decision. He was preparing to share it with the members of Congress and the rest of the world.

A conflict had been raging in Europe since Germany had declared war on Russia in August 1914. Although some Americans wanted the United States to enter the war, the president had promised that the country would remain neutral. Just months before his decision, Wilson had won the presidency with slogans such as "He kept us out of the war" and "War in the East, peace in the West, thank God for Wilson."

At 8:32 in the evening, the Speaker of the House, Champ Clark, hit the desk with his gavel and called the room to order: "Gentlemen, the president of the United States."

Wilson was sweating as he walked up to the podium. Everyone was cheering and clapping, but Wilson's hands were shaking as he put his notes down in front of him. Closing his eyes, he took a deep breath before looking at the audience.

Ever since he had taken the oath as president, Woodrow Wilson had been filled with a sense of the awesome responsibility that was his. He knew that the leadership and protection of the United States were in his hands. Especially now, when the world was on the brink of disaster, everyone would look to him to make the right choices. The decision he had made earlier in the day was probably the most important one he would make as president, and he prayed that it was the right one. He knew that it would hold sad consequences for millions of Americans but that eventually the world would be a better place because of their sacrifices.

Wilson began his speech: "Gentlemen of the Congress, I have called the Congress into extraordinary session because there are serious, very serious, choices of policy to be made, and made immediately which it was neither right nor constitutionally permissible that I should assume the responsibility of making."

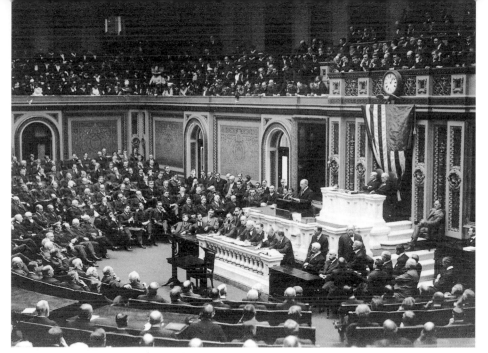

*Wilson asks a special session of Congress
to declare war against Germany.*

———————— ✧ ————————

The president's voice rose and fell as he spoke, and the audience applauded enthusiastically. Wilson outlined the reasons for his decision to call the Congress together and the dire implications of what he was going to ask. Finally, his voice took on a deeper solemnity as he got to the most important part of his speech. "With a profound sense of the solemn and even tragical character of the step I am taking and of the grave responsibilities which it involves, but in unhesitating obedience to what I deem my constitutional duty, I advise that the Congress declare the recent course of the Imperial German Government to be, in fact, nothing less than war against the Government and people of the United States."

President Wilson was asking Congress to declare war on Germany. The United States was about to enter the war in Europe.

CHAPTER ONE

A SOUTHERN BOYHOOD

"When you frame a sentence . . . do it as if you were loading a rifle. . . . Shoot with a single bullet and hit that thing alone."
—Dr. Wilson to his son Tommy

Thomas Woodrow Wilson, called Tommy as a boy, was used to the hardships of war. Born on December 28, 1856, in Staunton, Virginia, he had grown up during the Civil War (1861–1865), the conflict between the Northern and the Southern states.

At the heart of the conflict was the debate over slavery. At the time, many African Americans worked as slaves on Southern plantations. Southerners felt that their farms would not succeed without slave labor. But many people in the Northern states felt that slavery was wrong. Eventually, the Southern states broke away from the United States, or the Union, and formed their own nation, called the Confederacy. In April 1861, four-year-old Tommy Wilson,

Staunton, Virginia, was a bustling community of four thousand when Thomas Woodrow Wilson was born there in 1856.

then living with his family in Augusta, Georgia, watched as two thousand of his townsmen marched off to enlist in the Confederate army.

Tommy was third in a family of four children. He had two older sisters, Marion and Annie Josephine, and a younger brother, Joseph Jr. His parents were Dr. Joseph Wilson, a Presbyterian minister, and Janet "Jessie" Woodrow Wilson, who had emigrated from England at age seven. Both parents had Scottish and Scotch-Irish roots.

Tommy was too young to remember much about the Civil War, but some events made a lasting impression on him. For instance, in the middle of a sermon one Sunday, Dr. Wilson told his congregation to hurry to the ammunitions factory and set to work making supplies for the Confederate army. On another occasion, Dr. Wilson allowed the courtyard of his church to be used as a military

Uniformed Confederate soldiers were a familiar sight to young Tommy. His family lived in the South.

✧ ——————————————

prison camp. There, Tommy saw hundreds of frightened and wounded Union soldiers guarded by Confederate troops. Tommy and his cousin often sneaked into the camp to speak to the prisoners. When Mrs. Wilson discovered what they were doing, she scolded them, saying that the Union soldiers were bad men.

As the war raged on, famine and hardship became a reality. The Wilson family once ate soup made with weeds because there were no fresh vegetables to be had. The war ended with a Northern victory in 1865. Eight-year-old Tommy saw the Confederate president, Jefferson Davis, escorted by Union troops in Augusta. Davis had been taken prisoner by the Union. As Northern soldiers marched him down Augusta's main street, tearful townspeople waved Confederate flags in support.

LIFE'S LESSONS

Tommy's parents doted on their oldest son. Mrs. Wilson was shy and reserved. She was overprotective of Tommy at times, often coddling him and warning him about exaggerated dangers. "I remember how I clung to her till I was a

Tommy drew this picture of a steam locomotive in action when he was no more than four years old.

◇

great big fellow," Wilson later said, "but love of the best womanhood came to me and entered my heart through those apron strings."

Many schools had closed during the Civil War, so Dr. Wilson began teaching Tommy on his own at home. Tommy was later enrolled in a private school, Professor Joseph Derry's academy. Professor Derry taught Tommy to read, but his real teacher was his father.

Dr. Wilson believed that a boy's education should not be confined to the classroom but should consist of life experiences. So Dr. Wilson took Tommy on tours of local industries, such as the cotton mill, the ironworks, and the steel foundry. He explained the step-by-step process of how cotton was manufactured, how iron was processed, and how steel was produced. Dr. Wilson and Tommy also shared many hours together playing chess and billiards.

Dr. Wilson also taught his son the beauty of language. Before becoming a minister, Dr. Wilson had taught rhetoric, the art of speaking and writing effectively, at various colleges in Virginia. Together, he and Tommy would read great historical speeches and then rewrite them, attempting to improve the language and make the ideas clearer and more concise. Dr. Wilson never allowed his son to use a word incorrectly. He insisted that every idea be expressed in perfect English.

Evenings at the Wilson household often found the family in prayer or singing hymns together. Some nights,

✧ ———————

Jessie Woodrow Wilson, Tommy's mother

Tommy's father,
Joseph Ruggles Wilson
———————— ✧

Tommy's two sisters, Marion and Annie Josephine, would sit sewing or knitting with their mother, while Tommy lay on the floor in front of the fire. The family listened as Dr. Wilson reading the works of famous authors such as Charles Dickens and Sir Walter Scott.

Although Tommy spent a lot of time with his family, he also had some close friends his own age. In 1868 he and some friends created an organization called the Lightfoot Club. Tommy offered his family's hayloft as a gathering place. He was immediately elected president of the club and was put in charge of drafting a constitution, which he did with a great deal of seriousness. As a mascot for the club, the boys used a drawing of a devil, which they found on an ad for deviled ham. They displayed the mascot when they played baseball against teams of other local boys.

Like most children, Tommy occasionally got into trouble. One time a circus came to town, and he decided to

*Once a traveling circus tempted Tommy
to skip school. He could not resist.*

———————————— ✧ ————————————

skip school to see the entertainment. He knew that when
he got back, Professor Derry was going to give him a
spanking. So he stopped at the cotton mill and stuffed his
pants with cotton. That way, he thought, the punishment
wouldn't hurt as much. But Professor Derry was aware of
this trick and hit his student extra hard through the cotton
in his trousers.

COLLEGE BOUND
In 1870, when Tommy was thirteen years old, the family
moved to Columbia, South Carolina. Dr. Wilson had
accepted a job there as a professor at a Presbyterian theo-
logical seminary—a school that trained young men to be
ministers. Meanwhile, Mrs. Wilson had inherited quite a

lot of money from her family. So the Wilsons were able to live very well, even though Dr. Wilson didn't make a lot of money as a professor.

Tommy was enrolled in another private school, Barnwell's School, run by Charles H. Barnwell. Tommy was one of fifty boys in the school. Although he was intelligent, he didn't do very well at the school. He found classes boring. But he learned a great deal on his own. He was an avid reader and digested books on history and political science. Tommy loved reading about the lives of great people in history. He considered the presidency of the United States to be a great profession.

Sometimes Dr. Wilson invited missionaries to speak at the seminary. These were people who had spent many years traveling around the world, preaching about God. They had fascinating stories to tell about their international travels. Tommy was invited to sit quietly while his father and the missionaries carried on deep discussions about religion, politics, and philosophy. Dr. Wilson also gave Tommy a key to the seminary library, where he spent hours reading the works of great Presbyterian thinkers and teachers. Sometimes, Tommy listened to his father lecture at the seminary.

Dr. Wilson hoped that his son would follow in his footsteps and eventually become a minister. With this hope in mind, Dr. Wilson enrolled Tommy at Davidson College, a small religious college in North Carolina. In the fall of 1873, sixteen-year-old Tommy set off on his own for the first time.

CHAPTER TWO

TO SCHOOL AND BACK

*"I intend to spare no trouble in gaining
complete command of my voice in
reading and speaking."*
—Woodrow Wilson

In September 1873, when Tommy arrived there, Davidson was not much of a college by modern standards. It consisted of a single building. The rooms for students were small, cramped, and cold. There was no running water. The students had to chop down trees to burn in the fireplaces and carry in water for drinking and bathing.

Tommy introduced himself to his classmates as Woodrow Wilson, not as Tommy or Thomas. Woodrow was his middle name and his mother's maiden name. He used it in her honor. He would be known as Woodrow Wilson for the rest of his life.

Wilson looked upon college life as an adventure. He was upset, however, when the dean reviewed his past schoolwork

Woodrow Wilson, age seventeen

and found that he lacked some necessary courses. To catch up with the other students, Wilson was required to take geography, mathematics, Latin, and Greek. He was put on probation until he had successfully passed these courses.

Wilson knew that complaining about the additional coursework wasn't going to get it accomplished. So he exerted extra effort in his studies. Even so, he was never much more than a C student. During his first college semester, he scored only a 74 percent in math. But he earned a 96 in English, and he did impress his professors with his speaking skills.

Davidson College had two debating clubs—organizations where students discussed and argued about important issues of the day. Debate topics included questions about slavery, the Civil War, and other recent political events. Wilson joined the Eumenean Club. He soon became known as one of the finest debaters the college had ever seen. He also found time to get involved in sports. He played center field on Davidson's baseball team.

In May 1874, at the end of Wilson's freshman year, he became ill with mononucleosis, a temporary blood disorder that makes a person very tired and sickly. To regain his strength and health, Wilson moved back in with his family, who by then had moved to Wilmington, North Carolina, where his father had taken a new job. Wilson was careful not to let his mind get lazy while he was home. He read many books from his father's well-stocked library. Wilson also enjoyed taking long, solitary walks through the woods surrounding the family home.

Wilson played baseball from a young age.

Dr. James McCosh

In the spring of 1875, Dr. James McCosh came to visit the Wilson family. McCosh was the president of Princeton University in Princeton, New Jersey. While staying with the Wilsons, he was impressed with the younger Wilson's intellect and his sharp mind. Before he left, McCosh told Dr. Wilson that he expected to see Woodrow at Princeton in the fall. The younger Wilson gladly accepted the invitation.

A GREAT DISCOVERY

When eighteen-year-old Woodrow Wilson entered Princeton University in September 1875, the Civil War had been over for ten years. But some students were still fighting the war in their minds. There were still bitter feelings between Northerners and Southerners, so the college arranged to keep the two factions apart as much as possible. Southerners were assigned to separate housing and dining facilities. Wilson, however, soon got tired of the students' ongoing discussions on the sole topic of the Civil War. He decided to leave the other students and room by himself in another part of the campus.

By then, Wilson's strength and health had returned. But it appeared that his academic schedule was going to be as tough at Princeton as it had been at Davidson. The reason was the same—he hadn't fulfilled the course requirements to meet the university's standards. Again, he was required to take extra classes in mathematics, Latin, and Greek. Wilson received only average grades during his first year at Princeton, and when names were posted for the honor roll, his was missing.

Although he didn't excel academically, Wilson did make a great discovery during his days at Princeton. One morning, he visited the university library to research a paper for English class. Browsing through the stacks, he saw several bound volumes of *Gentleman's Magazine,* a British political publication. Wilson became so absorbed in reading the magazine that he soon forgot why he had visited the library in the first place. One article especially piqued his interest. The writer declared that great orators, or public speakers, were the true leaders of the people. He went on to say that to become a great speaker, one had to possess two vital qualities: sincerity and honest conviction.

Wilson suddenly knew what he was going to do with his career. He would become a great public speaker and a great statesman—a U.S. senator. He would devote his life to improving the United States.

When Wilson went back to his room, he wrote a letter to his parents. His excitement poured onto the paper as he told them about his new vision for his life. Unfortunately, the Wilsons did not read the letter with the same level of excitement. Dr. Wilson was particularly disappointed that his son did not want to become a minister. "Oh, my boy," he wrote in reply, "how I wish you had entered the ministry, with all that genius of yours."

But Wilson had made up his mind, and nothing would stop him. From then on, everything he did was with this vision in mind. He was filled with a new sense of self-confidence, and he became very serious about his studies. He practiced his speaking skills by reading great political speeches aloud while walking in the woods near school. He announced to anyone who would listen that he would one day become a U.S. senator, representing the state where he was born. To make his point, Wilson had business cards printed with the words: Thomas Woodrow Wilson / Senator from Virginia.

When he returned home for vacations, Wilson listened carefully to his father's speech patterns. He tried to analyze his father's words. He noted when his father placed emphasis on certain words, and he wanted to know why. He also noted which words his father used to drive home an important point.

Wilson eventually turned his love of public speaking into publication. In 1878, during his senior year at Princeton, he published an article in a political journal called the *International Review*. Entitled "Cabinet Government in the United States," the article compared the English House of Commons with the U.S. government's congressional committees.

Wilson still enjoyed extracurricular activities. He played on the Princeton baseball team. He served as president of the school's baseball association and athletic commission. He also sang in the glee club.

Wilson, hat in hand, poses with other members of the Princeton dining club. They called themselves the Alligators.

In June 1879, Wilson graduated from Princeton, with the rank of 38th in a class of 105 students. His standing did not please Dr. Wilson, who had expected Wilson to be valedictorian, or head of the class. After gently scolding his son for not using his brain to full capacity, Dr. Wilson wanted to know what Wilson was going to do with the rest of his life. Dr. Wilson hadn't given up on his dream that Wilson would become a minister.

But Wilson's interests never swerved. He was going to be a statesman and the best orator he could be. The first step on the road to becoming a politician, Wilson felt, was to become a lawyer. So in the fall of 1879, Wilson enrolled at the University of Virginia Law School in Charlottesville.

CHAPTER THREE

STATESMAN IN TRAINING

"The profession I chose was politics. The profession I entered was the law. I entered the one because I thought it would lead to the other. Congress is full of lawyers."
—Woodrow Wilson

By attending the University of Virginia, Wilson was joining the company of past American greats such as the poet Edgar Allan Poe, as well as Thomas Jefferson and James Monroe, who had both been acclaimed statesmen and presidents of the United States. In fact, Jefferson had founded the college in 1825, a few miles from his home in Monticello. Jefferson's influence was all over the campus. He had designed the original campus complex and the Rotunda (a round, domed building). There were also several statues of Jefferson in university buildings and a Jefferson museum in the library. Wilson often walked past a house that Monroe had once occupied, and he lived near Poe's former residence.

The university's debating society was named the Jefferson Society, and Wilson joined the group soon after enrolling at school. He became president of the society in the spring of 1880 and immediately set about rewriting its constitution. Wilson's reputation as an exceptional debater soon spread, not only at the college but also throughout Charlottesville.

Wilson found the teachers at the University of Virginia exciting, but he found the law courses boring. He had little patience for all the facts he had to memorize to get good grades. "I wish now to record the confession," Wilson wrote to a friend, "that I am terribly bored by the noble study of Law sometimes, though in the main I am thoroughly satisfied with my choice of profession. . . . The excellent thing, the Law, gets as monotonous as that immortal article of food, hash, when served with such endless frequency." To make his years at the law school tolerable, Wilson put most of his energy into campus life, into reading political books, and into his first love, public speaking.

Wilson spent a lot of time at the library near the Rotunda (left), *reading the political books he loved.*

Reminders of Thomas Jefferson, such as this statue in the Rotunda, surrounded Wilson as he studied.

◇

In December 1880, Wilson became sick with a nervous stomach. As he had done at Davidson, he decided to leave the university and return home. But Wilson was not one to waste time. While recovering at home for a year and a half, he continued his course work on his own. He prepared to take the bar exam, the final test of his knowledge of the law.

AN ATLANTA LAWYER

Wilson finished his law studies in the spring of 1882. He passed his examinations and was admitted to the bar, which meant he could officially practice law. He decided to open his practice in Atlanta, Georgia, a thriving southern city. Wilson was confident that his business would do well there.

Before leaving for Atlanta, Wilson wrote to Edward I.
Renick, a classmate from law school. Wilson remembered
Renick as having a personality similar to his own, with an
interest in the same subjects. After reconnecting, they made
the decision to go into business together.

When Wilson arrived in Atlanta in June 1882, he found
that Renick had already rented them rooms in a boarding-
house. Renick had also found a possible office space.
Within a couple of weeks, Wilson and Renick had rented
the office and furnished it with a desk and a bookcase provided by Dr. Wilson. They had business cards printed:
Renick and Wilson, Attorneys at Law.

Ordinarily, a bustling city like Atlanta would need good
new lawyers. However, Wilson soon discovered that the city
already had about 250 lawyers. A couple of lawyers fresh
from school weren't going to do very well, he realized. So
he and Renick spent most of their time reading political
and history books and discussing current issues. Wilson
honed his speaking skills by reading poetry to his partner.
Fortunately, both Wilson and Renick were receiving small
allowances from their families. This money allowed them to
pay their rent and eat three meals a day.

Several months went by, but neither Wilson nor Renick
saw more than a handful of clients. Wilson grew impatient
waiting for clients to knock on the door. He was hungry
for firsthand experience practicing law. He decided to visit
the local courts, hoping to learn from some of the city's
more knowledgeable lawyers. But when he did, he was very
disappointed. He discovered that most of Atlanta's lawyers,
many of them well respected, were debating small cases
concerning minor crimes like stealing and trespassing. He

had imagined that smart, successful lawyers conducted important business, such as fighting for the civil rights of their clients and debating local laws.

Next, Wilson visited the state capitol building to watch Georgia's state senators at work. He truly lost heart upon hearing these supposedly intelligent and educated men speaking in ungrammatical sentences and using improper speech patterns. He felt that that these legislators, who were supposed to represent the American people, were doing a poor job of it.

——————————— ✧ ———————————

Wilson found that Atlanta, Georgia, was already full of lawyers, and Georgia's state legislators disappointed him.

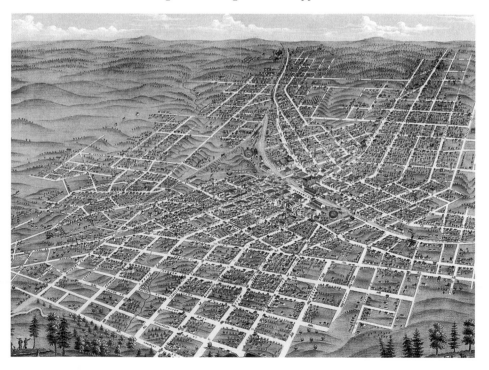

By the end of 1882, Wilson was compelled to take a long, hard look at the path his career was taking. He realized he would never be happy unless he led a life filled with intellectual pursuits. He also realized that he was wasting his time in Atlanta. Atlanta's citizens were not interested in politics or literature, he believed. They could never understand a cultured mind like his own. "Here," he wrote to his family, "the chief end of man is certainly to make money, and money cannot be made except by the most vulgar methods. The studious man is pronounced impractical and is suspected as a visionary."

Wilson's family didn't understand his dilemma. After he sent numerous letters home telling of his failure to begin a business, his father proclaimed: "That boy down in Atlanta still isn't earning a penny!"

Wilson finally decided that his desire for an intellectual life was in direct opposition to the practice of law. He needed a new profession—and he soon chose one. "My plain necessity, then, is some profession which will afford me a moderate support, favorable conditions for study, and considerable leisure; what better can I be, therefore, than a professor?"

Thus, Woodrow Wilson made the decision to abandon his law career and renew his studies. He enrolled as a graduate student of history and political science at Johns Hopkins University in Baltimore, Maryland. A flood of relief greeted his decision. He felt confident that an academic life would adequately nourish his intellect. He believed he would be happy and fulfilled in his career.

CHAPTER FOUR

NEW BEGINNINGS

*"Every one of his lectures [was] fascinating,
and held me spellbound; each was an almost
perfect essay in itself, well rounded and
with a distinct literary style."*
—William Starr Myers,
a former student of Wilson's

Woodrow Wilson couldn't wait for September 1883, when he would begin his graduate studies at Johns Hopkins University. Then, just as he was yearning to begin his academic life, Wilson fell in love.

The meeting came about quite by accident in the spring. Soon after his decision to begin graduate school, Wilson made a trip from Atlanta to Rome, Georgia. His mother owned some property there, and she wanted Wilson to act as her legal representative in selling it.

In Rome, Wilson attended a Sunday service in the Reverend Samuel Axson's little country church. It was there that he saw Ellen Louise Axson, the reverend's daughter. He thought she was the most beautiful, exotic creature on the planet. As soon as possible, he arranged to pay a visit to the family.

Wilson soon became acquainted with Ellen and made many more visits to Rome. They went on picnics and long walks and took boat rides and drives in the country. When they were apart, they wrote each other almost daily. Wilson was completely smitten with Ellen.

When September came, Wilson left for Baltimore to begin his studies. His train happened to stop at Asheville, North Carolina, before continuing on to Baltimore. When Wilson looked out the train window, he was shocked and

Ellen Axson

delighted to see Ellen sitting on the porch of a hotel. When he ran out to greet her, Ellen explained that her father was ill. She had been in New York, studying painting at the famous Art Students League. She was in Asheville waiting for the train home.

Wilson knew that he was meant to spend the rest of his life with this woman. He proposed to her there on the porch of the hotel. Ellen said yes. Weeks later, Wilson wrote to Ellen: "You are the only person in the world—except for the dear ones at home—with whom I do not have to act a part, to whom I do not have to deal out confidences cautiously. My salvation is in being loved."

INDEPENDENT STUDY

Despite his initial enthusiasm for graduate school, Wilson was no happier at Johns Hopkins than he had been at law school. After two months of attending classes, memorizing dry facts, and sitting through extra lectures after class, Wilson decided that he could not bear graduate school one day more. He made an appointment with Dr. Herbert Adams, his professor in international law, and told him of his dilemma.

To Wilson's delight, Adams gave him permission to conduct his studies on his own, as long as he could pass the exams at the end of the courses. He would not have to attend classes or extra lectures. He was responsible for studying at his own pace and on his own time. This process was not new to Wilson. He had been learning on his own since childhood, and he had passed his bar exams by studying at home. This approach seemed to be the way Wilson learned best.

This change made the rest of Wilson's stay at Johns Hopkins pleasant and successful. He did so well in his studies that he was awarded a fellowship to complete his second year, which meant that the university would pay his tuition.

TEACHER, AUTHOR, AND HUSBAND

In January 1885, Wilson accepted a position as associate professor of history and political science at Bryn Mawr College, an all-female school in Philadelphia, Pennsylvania. The position would begin in the fall of that year. Wilson took the job even though he hadn't finished the work for his graduate degree. To earn his diploma, he still needed to choose a topic of study and to write a dissertation—a long paper discussing that topic. He also needed to pass examinations. But Wilson was anxious to start teaching. He decided to put off completing his graduate work until a later time.

Also in January, Wilson saw the long-awaited publication of a book he had been writing in graduate school, *Congressional Government: A Study in American Politics.* The book increased his reputation in the academic community.

Then, on June 24, 1885, Woodrow Wilson married Ellen Axson. They moved to Philadelphia in August and rented a furnished room on the Bryn Mawr campus. They led a quiet life in Philadelphia, partly because they didn't have room to entertain but also because Wilson spent most of his free time reading and writing.

Ellen was quiet and reserved. Like her husband, she spent much of her free time reading. She read many books on history and political science so that she could better understand her husband's work. She eventually began proofreading his writing, and she later edited and rewrote many of his speeches.

Bryn Mawr, with its all-female student body, wasn't necessarily the best fit for Wilson. He had very narrow ideas about how women should be educated. Certainly, he thought women to be intelligent, but he felt they were more suited for marriage and motherhood than for academic pursuits. He also believed that women were too gentle for a field like political science, even though that's what he had come to Bryn Mawr to teach. Wilson constantly complained to Ellen about the dullness of his female students. "Teaching women relaxes one's mental muscles," he told her. "There is undoubtedly a painful absenteeism of mind."

Wilson's views were not unusual for the late nineteenth century. Many men of that era believed that women were only suited to be housewives and mothers. The law of Wilson's time stated that women were not allowed to vote or own property. Most educated women did not have jobs, except as teachers. In Wilson's era, very few women went to college at all. The students at Bryn Mawr were exceptions.

Given Wilson's views about women, it was surprising that he accepted the job at Bryn Mawr in the first place. Even more puzzling, he had had offers to teach at more prestigious men's colleges. Nevertheless, Wilson stayed at Bryn Mawr for the next three years. During these years, he spent most of his free time working on a new book about politics. He also published several articles in professional journals.

NEW CHALLENGES

Early on in Wilson's stay at Bryn Mawr, other staff members expressed concern that he did not have a graduate degree. He immediately wrote to Dr. Adams at Johns Hopkins, reminding him that he had left school before finishing his dissertation and asking for advice. Dr. Adams decided to accept Wilson's book, *Congressional Government,* in place of the required dissertation, but Wilson still had to take the required examinations. In May 1886, Wilson returned to Johns Hopkins to take rigorous exams, which lasted two days. He passed them all and proudly received his Ph.D. (doctor of philosophy) degree.

Meanwhile, the Wilson family was growing. One month earlier, in April 1886, Ellen had given birth to a baby girl, Margaret. The following year, on August 28, 1887, another daughter was born. They named her Jessie Woodrow.

Financially, these years were tough for the Wilson family. Wilson's salary was small, and it hadn't increased when he received his Ph.D. Money was scarce, and, with a growing family, Wilson constantly worried about how he would take care of them. Whenever the opportunity arose, Wilson earned extra money by speaking at political functions. He began to regret taking the job at Bryn Mawr, especially knowing that he could have received a larger salary elsewhere.

Fortunately, Ellen had received an inheritance from her father's estate, a sum of nearly $1,500, which was a great deal of money in 1887. Ellen used this money to cover the bills when Wilson's salary didn't go far enough. In April 1888, the Wilsons leased an eleven-room house near the college. Ellen used some of her money to buy furniture.

When Wilson was asked to join the faculty of Wesleyan University in Middletown, Connecticut, a school for men only, he jumped at the chance. "I have for a long time been hungry for a class of men," he wrote. His salary would be $2,500 a year—a significant increase over his salary at Bryn Mawr.

On September 1, 1888, the Wilsons moved to Middletown, where they rented a large house. When he wasn't teaching, Wilson devoted his time to writing. He made notes by hand and then transcribed them on the typewriter. He set aside a private study for his work and filled it from floor to ceiling with books. He decorated the

————————————— ✧ —————————————

Wilson was a new faculty member at Wesleyan University when this faculty photo was taken. He is third from the left in the front row.

One of Wilson's heroes, American statesman
Daniel Webster, addresses a crowd.

─────────────────── ✧ ───────────────────

walls with portraits of his heroes, including British prime
minister William Gladstone and American statesman Daniel
Webster. He also lectured at other East Coast universities,
including Johns Hopkins. Wilson's second book, *The State:
Elements of Historical and Practical Politics,* was published in
the fall of 1889.

Ellen fully supported and respected her husband's rou-
tine, and she made sure he had the privacy and quiet he
needed. She also had plenty of her own responsibilities. She
cared for her two young daughters and gave birth to a
third, Eleanor Randolph, called Nell, in October 1889.

CHAPTER FIVE

A RETURN TO PRINCETON

"It is plain what the nation needs as its affairs grow more and more complex. It needs efficient and enlightened men. The universities of the country must take part in supplying them."
—Woodrow Wilson

The next step in Woodrow Wilson's academic career came in 1890, when he accepted a professorship at Princeton University, his former school. The family moved again, arriving in Princeton in September. Their house was not yet ready, so they spent a few weeks living at the Nassau Hotel. In early November, the Wilsons moved into their new home.

At first, the three Wilson daughters did not attend a formal school. Instead, Ellen taught them herself every morning. She read aloud to them from Shakespeare's plays and from works by the great English poets. She told stories from Greek mythology and the works of the Greek philosophers. The Wilson sisters learned more from their mother

At first Ellen Wilson homeschooled her daughters,
Jessie and Margaret (left) and Eleanor (right).

than they probably would have in a traditional school. A few months after her fifth birthday, Nell, the youngest, was already able to read. Later, the Wilson girls were enrolled at a private school. The headmistress there told Ellen that her daughters were "the most intelligent, the best-trained, and the most thorough pupils" she had ever seen.

Wilson continued teaching and writing. He gave lectures with eloquence, clarity, and flair. Students thought he was fascinating. "It may be frankly stated here that, after experience with some very great teachers, I consider Wilson the greatest class-room lecturer I have ever heard," remarked William Starr Myers, a student of Wilson's who went on to become a professor himself. Wilson was repeatedly voted Princeton's most popular professor. He was also the school's most highly paid professor.

Other universities and colleges relentlessly tried to lure him away from Princeton. In 1898 finances at the school grew short, and all the professors had to take a salary cut. Afraid that Wilson would leave for another school if his salary were reduced, a small group of wealthy graduates offered to supplement his pay if he promised to stay.

By 1902 Woodrow Wilson had published nine books and more than thirty articles while holding down a demanding teaching schedule. He had become prominent in political circles, both academic and public. He was one of the most highly regarded political scientists in the nation. So, in June 1902, when Princeton's trustees were looking to elect the next president of the university, Woodrow Wilson was their unanimous choice.

Wilson was offered $6,000 a year, a huge salary at that time. He was extremely pleased and excited by the appointment, remarking, "I feel the weight of the responsibility, but I am glad to say that I do not feel it as a burden. I feel like a new prime minister." The election also marked an important crossroad in Wilson's career—for it signaled the end of his work as a scholar and the beginnings of his life as a politician.

Before starting his new position, Wilson took a trip to Europe with Ellen. This would be their first time traveling a long distance together, and they were very excited. The Wilson daughters, by then in their teens, stayed with Madge Axson, Ellen's cousin, while their parents were overseas.

Wilson and Ellen toured England and Scotland, visiting art museums and castles in both countries. They also visited France and Switzerland before returning home in late August 1902.

PRINCETON'S NEW PRESIDENT

In 1902 Princeton did not carry the prestigious name that it does in modern times. In Wilson's time, the university was known as a country club for sons of wealthy alumni (former students). The course load was easy. Many undeserving students received high grades because their families had donated money to the university. The professors were overworked and underpaid. Many of them were of poor quality.

Big Ben (left) is a prominent landmark in England, where the Wilson's European tour started.

As president of Princeton, Wilson had ambitious plans for the university.

Wilson's goal was to make Princeton a great university by expanding its course offerings, raising its academic standards, and improving the quality of its professors. He wanted to add more science classes, buy new equipment, and pay professors more money. He also felt that new teaching methods would be crucial to raising the university's standards. Specifically, he wanted to emphasize *thinking* instead of memorizing facts from textbooks.

Wilson detailed many of these reforms on October 25, 1902, when he was sworn in as president of the university at an elaborate ceremony. Several prestigious men attended the ceremony, including J. P. Morgan, one of the wealthiest bankers in the country, author Mark Twain, and African American leader Booker T. Washington.

Mark Twain (left), *J. P. Morgan* (center), *and Booker T. Washington*
(right) *attended Wilson's swearing-in as president of Princeton.*

Wilson also discussed his ideas at his first meeting with the university trustees. He informed them that the overall status of the college was critical. He said they would need to raise a lot of money to put Princeton on the list of the top ten colleges in the United States. The trustees were shocked when Wilson estimated that the school would need $12.5 million to fulfill this goal. He appealed to wealthy trustees and alumni to make pledges of $100,000 each, to be paid over three years.

While this was an exciting time in Wilson's career, he also suffered a personal loss. His father died in 1903, and his passing deeply affected Wilson. He had lost his mentor, his hero, and his friend. He grieved the loss for many months.

AN OFFER FROM THE DEMOCRATS

Wilson's years as Princeton's president were productive ones. Many of his reforms were successfully enacted during this period. In addition to his duties as president, he was kept busy giving addresses at many political and educational events across the country. When he wasn't giving speeches, he wrote articles for magazines such as the *Independent, Atlantic Monthly, North American Review,* and *Harper's Weekly.*

In early 1910, while Wilson was hard at work at Princeton, some big names in the New Jersey Democratic Party were having a quiet luncheon. One of the main topics of conversation was the upcoming election for governor of New Jersey. The politicians were considering which person to nominate for the job. Wilson's name was mentioned, and a deep discussion ensued about his political views, his desire to do things his own way, and his availability to run for office.

In July, Wilson was invited to an afternoon conference at the Lawyers' Club in Newark, New Jersey. There he met with a group of political leaders, who asked him two important questions: First, if elected governor, would he set about tearing down the existing Democratic organization and replace it with one of his own? Second, what were his views on legalizing the sale of liquor in the state? The latter issue was one of immense concern to citizens. At the time, it was illegal to sell beer, wine, or any other liquor in New Jersey. Many taxpayers wanted this law changed.

Wilson commented on the first question by saying, "The last thing I should think of would be building up a [political] machine of my own." He assured the men at the conference that as long as the party leaders backed his policies and gave him a certain amount of freedom, he would support the Democratic organization as it was. Wilson was undecided about legalizing the sale of liquor. He told the men that on that issue, he would go along with the majority of voters. The politicians seemed satisfied with Wilson's answers. In September 1910, Woodrow Wilson was nominated as the Democratic candidate for the governorship of New Jersey.

It was once again time for Wilson to move on in his career. He gave his resignation to the leaders of Princeton. They congratulated him on his new opportunity and wished him well.

In this cartoon, Wilson wears his Princeton cap and gown to ride the symbolic Democratic Party donkey. He was known as the Schoolmaster in Politics.

CHAPTER SIX

FROM GOVERNOR TO PRESIDENT

"Know your people and you can lead them; study your people and you may know them."
—Woodrow Wilson

By 1910, when Wilson was nominated as the Democratic candidate for governor of New Jersey, the Republicans had been in control of the state's government for fifteen years. The Democrats felt it was high time they took over.

The main Democratic leader was James "Big Jim" Smith, a man who worked in politics mainly for personal power and financial gain. In fact, the state Democratic Party was riddled with such men, called bosses. That was the one aspect of the party that made Wilson cautious about accepting the nomination. He didn't want to become a puppet of Smith and the other bosses.

When Wilson had stated his views at the Lawyers' Club, he had asked the party to give him some freedom to run

the government as he saw fit. He was assured that he would
be allowed to do so. In actuality, Smith was just "yessing"
him. He planned to get Wilson into office, then crack down
hard and make Wilson do his bidding. But Smith didn't re-
alize how strong willed and stubborn Wilson could be.

While Smith was raising thousands of dollars for ex-
penses, fifty-three-year-old Wilson threw himself into the
campaign with enthusiasm. He raced around the state,
speaking on street corners and in town squares. He spoke
about preventing election fraud, protecting workers, and
keeping big businesses from growing too powerful—ideas
that did not sit well with Smith and the other bosses.

Wilson (center) *shakes hands with supporters after accepting
the Democratic Party's nomination.*

Big Jim desperately tried to control what Wilson was saying. But he soon realized that his attempts were futile. Wilson was going to say what he believed, and no one was going to change that. In all his speeches, Wilson expressed the same theme—that he was a man of the people.

On Election Day in November, Woodrow Wilson was elected governor of New Jersey by a large majority. Ellen wrote to a friend, "Certainly it is 'a famous victory.' The size of it almost takes one's breath away."

Rather than move to the state capital of Trenton, about fifteen miles away, the Wilsons decided to stay in Princeton. But they did move to a new house. Wilson, Ellen, and their daughters spent several weeks sorting through and throwing out twenty years' worth of possessions. They worked so hard that Ellen swore she would never save a thing in the future. They left Wilson's book-lined study until the last day, then they packed boxes and boxes of books and papers.

On January 17, 1911, Woodrow Wilson was sworn in as governor of New Jersey. The new house in Princeton was not yet ready, so the Wilsons spent several weeks living at the Princeton Inn, in three rooms filled to overflowing with boxes. By then, Margaret had her own apartment in New York City, where she was studying singing. Jessie worked in Philadelphia at a settlement house, an organization that helped poor women. Nell commuted daily by train from Princeton to the Pennsylvania Academy of Fine Arts.

Wilson was proud of his wife and daughters, although he admitted that fatherhood wasn't easy. When a journalist asked him, "Governor Wilson, have you been taught most by your wife? Or by your three daughters?" he replied: "From

Wilson's daughters Jessie (standing) *and Eleanor*
✧ ————————————

Mrs. Wilson, not only have I learned much but have gained something of a literary reputation. Whenever I need a poetic quotation she supplies it, and in this way I acquire the fame of possessing a complete anthology of poetry. From my daughters, however, I have learned what every parent knows of himself—that I do not know how to raise children."

AN IMMEDIATE SUCCESS

From his first day as governor, Wilson assured the citizens of New Jersey that he, not the bosses, was the responsible leader of the Democratic Party. He had every intention of fulfilling his promises to the voters. The door to his office was always open to the public. He wrote speeches using clear and simple language so that even uneducated people could understand what he was saying.

Wilson's work as governor of New Jersey was impressive. His first priority was to reform the procedures governing state elections. He pushed for laws to prevent election fraud and to keep big businesses from using their money and power to put their own candidates into office. He also worked to create a public utilities commission. This commission had the power to control the finances of utility companies—businesses that supplied necessities such as water, telephone service, and electric power. The law kept the companies from charging customers too much money. Wilson also helped working people by creating an employers' liability act. Under this law, employers were required to make payments to workers who were injured on the job.

The voters recognized Wilson's sincerity and honesty and loved him for it. When news of Wilson's achievements and popularity in New Jersey hit the national headlines, people began to say that a man like him would make a great president. Thousands of citizens wrote letters to his office, pledging votes and support if he decided to seek the job. It wasn't long before he was considered the most likely Democratic candidate for president in the next election.

WILSON FOR PRESIDENT

Spurred on by his popularity, Wilson agreed to run for president. He believed the country was in need of a change. The current president, Republican William Howard Taft, favored big business over the common citizen. In contrast, Wilson believed that businesses held too much power.

Taft was running for reelection. Another candidate was Theodore Roosevelt, who had already served as president

Wilson faced two opponents with previous experience as president, William Howard Taft (left), the incumbent, and Theodore Roosevelt (right).

————————————— ✧ —————————————

before Taft took office. Roosevelt had served as a Republican, but he now belonged to the Progressive Party, which stood for strong social and economic reforms.

Wilson hit the campaign trail in May 1911, after the New Jersey legislature finished its session. Riding by train, he began a national tour to let people all over the country know who he was and what he stood for. The trip was an enormous success. He traveled more than eight thousand miles, visiting cities between New York and San Francisco and giving more than thirty major speeches.

Wilson called his ideas the New Freedom. He explained to voters that he wanted to boost the U.S. economy. He wanted to help consumers by lowering taxes on goods imported into the United States. He also wanted to reform the nation's banking system and to make sure big business didn't gain too much power.

By the time Wilson returned to New Jersey, campaign contributions had begun to roll in. William McCombs, a former student of Wilson's at Princeton, became one of his most important aides. McCombs opened large campaign offices on Broadway in New York City. From there, he mailed out thousands of copies of Wilson's speeches to cities around the country.

Wilson crisscrossed the country, making speeches to voters.

THE DEMOCRATIC CANDIDATE

On July 2, 1912, the National Democratic Convention nominated Woodrow Wilson for president of the United States. He was now a national figure. What little privacy he had been able to eke out before his nomination was gone. "The life I am leading now can't keep up," Wilson wrote to a friend later that month. "Not a moment am I left free to do what I would. I thought last night that I should go crazy with the strain and confusion of it."

Throughout the summer, letter carriers delivered bags of mail to the Wilson summer home, located in Sea Girt on the Jersey shore. Ellen read all the letters and answered those that she thought needed a response. Many letters were from staunch Wilson supporters. These, Ellen showed

Supporters throng Sea Girt, Wilson's private home on the Jersey shore. Wilson is seated on a chair at far right.

*Ellen Wilson managed his campaign mail and
kept negative letters away from him.*

---

to her husband, especially at times when his self-confidence seemed to be failing. Some letters were from people who disliked Wilson. These, Ellen immediately threw into the trash, before her husband could see them. The negative letters depressed her greatly. "She walks around in a dream," Jessie wrote to Margaret about their mother. "Nothing but an article about Father can galvanize her into attention.... Everything against him makes her sick. It is dreadful."

On Election Day, November 4, 1912, the family gathered at their home in Princeton. Wilson voted in the morning and then had dinner with some friends. In those years, there were no radios or televisions to report the election results. Instead, at ten o'clock in the evening, a messenger arrived at the Wilsons' front door. He handed Ellen a written message called a telegraph. It said that Woodrow Wilson had just been elected the twenty-eighth president of the United States.

Wilson won the election with 435 of 531 electoral votes. In addition to voting for president, U.S. citizens had cast their votes for congressmen that day. The Democrats had won back control of the U.S. Congress.

The Wilsons heard cheers on the streets, and when Wilson went outside, he was greeted by a crowd of students from nearby Princeton, joined by local residents. Someone carried a chair into the street. Wilson stood on the chair and gave his first speech as president-elect: "I have no feeling of triumph tonight, but a feeling of solemn responsibility. I know the great task ahead of me and . . . I look almost with pleading to you . . . to stand behind me. . . . I believe that a great cause has triumphed for the American people. I know what we want, and we will not get it through a single man or a single session of Congress, but through a long process extending through the next generation."

A few weeks later, the Wilson family said tearful good-byes to their friends and neighbors in New Jersey. They packed up their belongings and left for Bermuda—for a brief rest before beginning their new lives in the White House.

CHAPTER SEVEN

THE NEW FREEDOM

"There is no other Navy in the world that has to cover so great an area of defense as the American Navy, and it ought in my judgement to be incomparably the greatest Navy in the world."
—Woodrow Wilson

On a beautiful sunny day, March 4, 1913, Woodrow Wilson was sworn in as the twenty-eighth president of the United States, with Ellen and his daughters by his side. In his inaugural address, he called for reform in the federal government. He described pervasive wastefulness in government and criticized people who used the government for their own selfish purposes. He also held a news conference—the first ever by a president. At the conference, he discussed his policies with newspaper reporters, who then relayed the ideas to readers across the country.

Facts about the Decade 1910–1920

- The average family income was $1,267.

- The cost of a new car was $390.

- A loaf of bread cost 7¢, a gallon of milk cost 35¢, and a gallon of gas cost 14¢.

- Erector sets, Tinkertoys, Lincoln Logs, and Ouija boards were popular toys.

- Popular cars included Chevrolets, Studebakers, and Packards.

- Popular songs included "Over There," "Pack Up Your Troubles in Your Old Kit Bag," "Keep the Home Fires Burning," and "Oh, How I Hate to Get Up in the Morning."

- Only one out of every one thousand couples got divorced.

- New inventions included the electric hair dryer and the refrigerator.

- The average life expectancy was 54.4 years.

- Popular products were Carnation milk, Ivory soap, Listerine, Tootsie Rolls, Planters peanuts, Campbell's soup, and Columbia records.

A 1913 Chevrolet

*Crowds gather for Wilson's inauguration
at the U.S. Capitol in Washington, D.C.*

———————————— ✦ ————————————

Wilson quickly set about implementing his promises of
the New Freedom. In 1909 Congress had passed the Payne-
Aldrich Tariff Act, a law that raised taxes on hundreds of
imported products. Wilson felt that this law was unreason-
able. It led to high prices for consumers, even for critical
items such as food and clothing. Wilson worked to pass a
new law, the Underwood Tariff Act. It lowered taxes on imported items and allowed necessary items, such as wool,
shoes, coal, lumber, eggs, milk, wheat, iron, and steel, to be
imported into the United States without any tax. On
September 9, 1913, the tariff bill passed in the Senate by a
vote of forty-four to thirty-seven.

Wilson also believed that the nation's banking system needed strengthening. At the time, all banks in the United States operated separately. The president thought it would be better if one main organization, called the Federal Reserve System, guided the banks and controlled the nation's money supply. In December 1913, Congress passed the Federal Reserve Act. This law created twelve Federal Reserve Banks, organized under one central office. The law required all American banks to join the new system.

Finally, Wilson believed that some big businesses held too much power. These businesses had complete control over certain industries, such as oil, steel, or railroads—a situation called a monopoly or a trust. The businesses could set high prices and force smaller firms to shut down.

A political cartoon from the late nineteenth century shows how monopolies control Uncle Sam, Congress, and the American people. Wilson agreed with the cartoon's message.

Wilson worked to pass the Clayton Antitrust Act, which helped break up these trusts and monopolies.

"A SCOTCH-IRISHMAN KNOWS HE IS RIGHT"

Woodrow Wilson was a storehouse of new ideas and plans. But he often thought that only his ideas were the right ones, and he felt disappointed when someone disagreed with him. He was very stubborn and never compromised. "A Scotch-Irishman knows he is right," Wilson was fond of saying.

At work, he tended to be quiet and serious. People meeting him for the first time often found him shy and aloof. He spent a lot of time in thought and was uncomfortable in social situations. At home, though, Wilson enjoyed a warm social life with his family. In fact, although they were in their twenties, all the Wilson daughters lived in the White House with their parents. A suite of rooms on the second floor served as living quarters. The Wilsons had fun as a family. Margaret, Jessie, and Nell tended to bring out their father's lighter side. Wilson enjoyed playing billiards, so Ellen had a billiards room set up in the White House. Wilson also played golf, but not very well.

Sometimes, the Wilson daughters liked to play practical jokes on visitors who toured the White House. One of the three would tag onto the end of a tour group and complain to the other tourists about how poorly the president was running the country. The shocked tourists had no idea that they were listening to one of the Wilson daughters.

Ellen Wilson liked to tend the White House garden. She arranged for rosebushes and trees to be planted there. She was also a talented painter and was delighted to find a room with a skylight in the White House attic. She turned this room into her studio, setting up her easel and paints. The sun shined through the skylight and brightened the room. Ellen set aside another room for displaying arts and crafts produced by poor women from mountainous regions of the United States. These items were sold to visitors on White House tours.

Ellen was also active in charities. One time, she convinced government officials to go with her to visit run-down sections of Washington, D.C., home to many African Americans. After seeing the crowded, unsanitary living conditions, senators passed an act that helped provide decent housing for hundreds of Washington residents. One reporter wrote: "Mrs. Wilson has done more good in Washington in four months than any other President's wife [has] ever done in four years—[she has] completely changed the conditions of life for 1,200 people."

WEDDINGS IN THE WHITE HOUSE

Ellen and her daughters spent the summer of 1913 vacationing in New Hampshire. There, Ellen became involved in local artists' groups. She hosted discussions and dinners on behalf of the arts community. Wilson was too busy to join his family in New Hampshire, except for a week in July. He missed them dearly, especially his wife, but he often read about her arts activities in the newspaper.

The couple sent nearly one hundred letters to each other during this period. Wilson wrote to Ellen: "Bless you, how everybody up there will love and admire you before the summer is over. The glimpses you give me of what you are doing enable me to see just how charming and natural and genuine a friend and neighbor you are making of yourself.

No President but myself had exactly the right sort of wife! I am certainly the most fortunate man alive!"

The country learned that summer that Jessie Wilson had secretly gotten engaged to Francis (Frank) Sayre, an attorney in New York City. Jessie and Frank had met when a cousin of the Wilsons' introduced them at a family weekend. Now the White House would host a wedding. People throughout the country were excited. In October, Ellen and her daughters began to prepare for the event. Jessie and Frank were married on November 25, 1913, with a big wedding in the White House.

———————————— ✧ ————————————

President and Mrs. Wilson, with Frank Sayre (the groom) beside her, stand behind Jessie (the bride in the white veil). On either side of the bride are her sisters, Margaret (left) and Eleanor (right).

Soon after Jessie's wedding, Nell announced her engagement to William McAdoo, Wilson's secretary of the treasury. William was twenty-six years older than Nell and was the father of six children. His wife had died shortly before he and Nell met. Her parents were not happy about the marriage. They thought William was too old for Nell.

But she was determined to marry him anyway. The wedding took place on May 7, 1914. It was a simple affair, with only close family friends and relatives invited.

✧ ————————————
President Woodrow Wilson

JOY TURNS TO SADNESS

By the spring of 1914, Ellen had not been feeling well for several months. At first she tried to hide her condition from her family. When she finally collapsed on the floor of their bedroom, Wilson called in the doctor. A team of physicians determined that Ellen had Bright's disease, a chronic inflammation of the kidneys. The disease was incurable. In July, Ellen's spirits were lifted a little by the news that Jessie was expecting a baby. But by August, Ellen was bedridden.

Wilson spent as much time as he could by Ellen's bedside. On August 6, the doctor took Wilson downstairs into a private room. He said that Ellen would live only a few more hours. Wilson then gave his daughters the sad news. Ellen died peacefully at five o'clock in the evening with her husband clasping her hand to his chest. He was bereft and brokenhearted. "Oh my God," he cried out. "What am I to do?"

Fifty-four-year-old Ellen Wilson was buried next to her father and mother at Myrtle Hill Cemetery in Rome, Georgia. Wilson went into a deep depression afterward. He felt lost and terribly alone. Although he had three daughters, they couldn't take the place of Ellen, who had provided him with so much love and support. He went into seclusion in the White House, but he continued to fulfill his responsibilities as president. He had little choice. A global crisis was awaiting his attention.

CHAPTER EIGHT

THE WAR TO END ALL WARS

"The people here [Germans] are firmly
convinced that we [Americans] can be
slapped, insulted, and murdered with absolute
impunity. If war comes . . . it will be because
we are totally unprepared and Germany
feels that we are impotent."
—Colonel Edward M. House,
American ambassador to Germany

By early 1914, Europe had become a hotbed of tension. Two distinct factions were on the verge of war: the Central Powers, consisting primarily of Germany and Austria-Hungary, and the Allied Powers, made up of Britain, France, and Russia. The conflict arose due to their alliances, the rivalries between their royal and ruling families, and a mutual distrust between the two groups.

The deciding blow was struck on June 28, 1914, when an assassin with ties to Serbia killed the Austrian crown

Archduke Franz Ferdinand
—————————— ✧

prince, Archduke Franz Ferdinand. Austria-Hungary declared war on Serbia, and Germany backed Austria-Hungary. Russia, a Serbian ally, immediately mobilized for war. On August 1, 1914, Germany declared war on Russia. Two days later, Germany declared war on France. Germany then invaded Belgium, which offered the shortest route to Paris, the French capital. With the invasion of Belgium, Britain declared war on Germany. The Great War (later called World War I) soon engulfed all of Europe.

NEUTRAL TERRITORY

Woodrow Wilson didn't have a great deal of experience with foreign policy. He had appointed a few experienced men to serve as ambassadors to the European countries, believing that diplomacy—goodwill and politeness—was all that was needed in matters of foreign relations. He felt the United States could remain neutral in the overseas conflict. After all, didn't the United States have enough to deal with on its own soil? Besides that, the European conflict confused Wilson. He wasn't sure who the aggressor was. Even if the United States wanted to take sides, it would be difficult to decide whether to back the Allied Powers or the Central Powers.

On August 19, 1914, Wilson presented a speech to the Senate, arguing for neutrality: "My Fellow Countrymen: I suppose that every thoughtful man in America has asked himself, during these last troubled weeks, what influence the European war may exert upon the United States. . . . The effect of the war on the United States will depend upon what American citizens say and do. Every man who really loves America will act and speak in the true spirit of neutrality, which is the spirit of impartiality and fairness and friendliness to all concerned."

As the months wore on, however, the conflict in Europe began to affect the U.S. economy, especially in the area of foreign trade. Britain would not allow foreign merchant ships to trade with Germany, which restricted U.S. and European trade. As time went on, the economic situation grew more severe. Wilson was no longer sure he could keep the country out of the war.

Eventually, Wilson began to feel emotionally drawn to Britain and the Allied Powers. He learned that Germany had been particularly ruthless, especially with its invasion of Belgium. He felt that the German leaders did not understand the difference between good and evil and had no faith in God.

Most Americans shared Wilson's feelings. Although few Americans wanted to get involved in the war overseas, the majority of citizens backed the Allies as the "good guys." Americans with German or Austrian roots were divided in their loyalties, however. Many of them supported the Allied cause, but others supported their home countries. This division of loyalty concerned

Wilson. He firmly believed that the entire country had to stand together in support of neutrality.

STOP SINKING OUR SHIPS, OR ELSE!

German U-boats, or submarines, patrolled the waters around Great Britain, attacking merchant ships and sometimes threatening passenger ships. In February 1915, Wilson sent a message to the German government. Should German vessels harm any American ship on the high seas, he warned, the United States would take any

———————————— ✧ ————————————

German U-boats sank numerous merchant and passenger ships.

measures necessary to protect the lives of its citizens. Wilson asked Germany to consider the waters around Great Britain "neutral seas" and to leave passenger ships unharmed.

By April, it was obvious that Germany had no intention of honoring Wilson's request. In an address to a joint session of Congress, Wilson condemned Germany's actions: "It is my duty to say to the Imperial German Government that if it is still its purpose to prosecute relentless and indiscriminate warfare against vessels of commerce by the use of submarines . . . the Government of the United States is at last forced to the conclusion that there is but one course it can pursue; this Government can have no choice but to sever diplomatic relations with the Government of the German Empire altogether."

Hopes for neutrality were weakening. Finally, the Germans committed an act that left neutrality hanging by a mere thread. On May 1, the British passenger ship *Lusitania* left New York on its way to Britain. On May 7, with the coast of Ireland in sight, German U-boat *U 20* torpedoed the ship. It sank in eighteen minutes, taking with it 1,195 lives—123 of them American men, women, and children.

Americans were outraged. The German government apologized, explaining that it thought the *Lusitania* was a warship carrying ammunition to the British. But Wilson told Germany that apologies could never make up for the sorrow Americans were feeling. Germany was treading in deep water, Wilson said, and the United States wouldn't tolerate its acts of piracy much longer.

Despite the public's outrage, Wilson continued to promote the philosophy of neutrality. He reasoned that

The successful German U-boat attack on the Lusitania
was headline news across the United States.

✧

although 123 American citizens had been killed in the
Lusitania tragedy, millions more would die if the United
States entered the war. But many Americans had changed
their minds about neutrality. Many people, especially those
whose family members or friends had been killed on
the *Lusitania,* publicly demanded that the United States
retaliate against Germany.

"HE KEPT US OUT OF WAR"

Wilson found that he missed Ellen dearly during this stressful time, not only for the love she had showered upon him but also for the support she had offered during such trying situations. He began to long for new love, and when a friend brought a female guest to tea, Wilson hoped that she would be the next woman in his life.

Edith Bolling Galt was a young and pretty widow who had taken over her husband's jewelry business after he died. After she and Wilson met, they fast became friends. They spent a great deal of time together throughout the spring and summer of 1915 and were married on December 18, 1915.

———————————— ✧ ————————————

*While war loomed, Wilson's marriage to Edith Bolling Galt
(below right) breathed new life into the Wilson White House.*

*Campaign posters for Wilson's second term as president
list his accomplishments during his first term.*

Wilson was approaching the last year of his presidential
term. He seriously questioned whether he should run for
reelection. The tensions in Europe and the death of his first
wife had left him drained. He was worn out by the burden
of making decisions for the country at such a crucial time
in history. He was also tired of holding to his philosophy of
neutrality when a growing number of people had started to
disagree with him. But he decided to run for a second term
anyway. "He kept us out of war" was his campaign slogan.

Wilson's opponent for the presidency was Republican Charles Evans Hughes, a former New York governor and a judge on the Supreme Court. Hughes had resigned from the Court to run his campaign. Wilson, on the other hand, felt that he couldn't put his energy into a large campaign in light of the serious situation facing the nation. He felt that he belonged at his desk, not traveling around the country talking to voters. So Wilson did very little campaigning, and as Election Day approached, he expected to lose the race.

On November 11, Election Day, Wilson boarded a train to attend the christening of his grandchild, Ellen Wilson McAdoo, Nell's daughter. Thinking he had lost the election, he felt relieved. Then the conductor, much to Wilson's shock, congratulated him on his victory. Woodrow Wilson would serve as president for another four years.

CHAPTER NINE

JOINING THE ALLIES

"I have called Congress into extraordinary session because there are serious, very serious, choices of policy to be made."
— Woodrow Wilson

By the beginning of 1917, it was obvious that the war in Europe was edging closer to North America. German submarines continued to attack merchant ships, including American vessels. Germany continued to ignore American requests and warnings. U.S. citizens were becoming more and more impatient with Germany's actions.

Then, on January 16, 1917, the German foreign minister, Arthur Zimmermann, sent a secret note to a German ambassador in Mexico City. The note never made it to Mexico because British agents intercepted it. In this short note, the Germans asked Mexico, the southern neighbor of the United States, to serve as a military base for war with the United States.

With war at the nation's doorstep, Wilson and his advisers realized that neutrality was no longer possible. The United States was forced to take action. On February 3, Wilson announced to Congress that the United States was formally severing diplomatic relations with Germany.

On March 4, Wilson announced that all U.S. merchant ships were to be armed for protection from the enemy. Twenty-eight days later, Wilson asked Congress to declare war on Germany, explaining that "the world must be made safe for democracy." He went on to outline the ruthless actions of the German government—its lies and its betrayals. He also spoke about his dream for peace and his hope that the United States could have stayed out of the war.

CALLING THE COUNTRY TO ARMS

In a State of the Union address on April 16, Wilson told the American people that the United States had entered into the war in Europe. He explained that the government was "rapidly putting our navy upon an effective war footing and [was] about to create and equip a great army."

Wilson explained that action had to be taken on the home front while troops were fighting in Europe. He called on farmers to grow additional crops to supply food for people at home, for the American military, and for citizens of other Allied countries. Some countries were on the edge of famine because their farms and fields had been bombed. He said that without enough food, the entire Allied defense would be crushed; the men would be too weak to fight. "Upon the farmers of this country . . . in large measure, rests the fate of the war and the fate of nations," he said.

FEED a FIGHTER
Eat only what you need –
Waste nothing –
That he and his family
may have enough
UNITED STATES FOOD ADMINISTRATION

*Posters like this one encouraged Americans to
support the war by conserving food.*

───────────────── ◇ ─────────────────

Wilson asked women to take over in jobs on farms and in factories—jobs vacated by men who were needed in the military. The crops and materials the women produced would help feed, clothe, and equip the armed forces, Wilson explained. Wilson told miners that coal would be needed to fuel ships and factories, especially factories that made weapons and ammunition. He explained that he had asked Congress to provide money to build more ships and submarines.

*Boys fill in as coal miners for their fathers, uncles,
and older brothers who are off to war.*

———————————— ✧ ————————————

Wilson called American factory workers an international
service army. He said that the workers had to increase pro-
duction and become more efficient. Although these workers
were not fighting in Europe, they were just as important as
soldiers to the success of the war. The equipment and supplies they produced would keep the Allies strong and help
them win the war.

On May 18, Wilson signed the Selective Draft Act. This
law required all men from twenty-one to thirty years of age
to register for military service. Also on May 18, Wilson
announced that he had "directed an expeditionary force of
approximately one division of regular troops under command of Major General John J. Pershing to proceed to

France at as early a date as practicable." Pershing left for France ten days later on the ship *Baltic*.

Citizens everywhere answered Wilson's call with enthusiasm and patriotism. Thousands of young men joined the armed forces, and other Americans contributed their energy on the home front. First Lady Edith Wilson pitched in, too. She led congressmen's wives in setting up sewing circles—groups of women who made clothing for the soldiers fighting in Europe.

────────────── ✧
Major General John J. Pershing

Fighting in the Trenches

World War I was particularly gruesome for foot soldiers. Armies defended their positions from trenches—long, deep ditches that zigzagged along the front lines. Often, the distance between enemy trenches was less than thirty yards. Soldiers lived in the trenches for days or weeks at a time. They stood guard with loaded rifles, knowing that the enemy might rush their trenches or begin firing at any moment. A soldier who raised his head above the top of a trench might be immediately hit by an enemy bullet. The goal of both sides was to hit the enemy's trenches with mortar shells, killing all the men inside and destroying the trenches completely.

Trenches smelled awful because they were filled with rotting corpses—during intense fighting, there was no chance to bury soldiers who had been killed. Rats ate at the dead bodies and spread disease. There were no beds in the trenches—soldiers had to sleep in the dirt. There were no bathrooms or places to wash. When it rained, many trenches filled up with muddy water, which only increased the misery, filth, and disease.

Edith also bought a huge flock of sheep and let them graze on the White House grounds. The White House gardeners had been drafted into military service, so the sheep kept the lawn trimmed instead. Edith even hired local farmers to shear the sheep. She then auctioned off ninety-eight pounds of wool and donated the money, more than $50,000, to the Red Cross.

THE WORK OF WAR AND PEACE

By October 1917, several new U.S. warships were ready to be launched. The U.S. Navy had constructed a string of mines across the northern entrance to the North Sea, and the United States had won 200 out of 227 battles with German U-boats. In December 1917, the United States officially declared war on the Austro-Hungarian Empire. But the Germans were bombing London from airships and shelling Paris from the outskirts of the city. An Allied victory did not look likely soon.

In Russia, revolutionaries had overthrown the government of Czar Nicholas II, but the new government continued fighting. Communists then took over the Russian government, and they revealed secret treaties that the former Russian government had hoped to keep hidden. The treaties described how the British, French, and Russians would divide up the war booty if the Allies were to win the war. This booty consisted of German money, art, and antiques.

The United States was outraged. These agreements showed the rest of the world, and especially the Americans, that the Allies were not fighting to make the world safe from unscrupulous governments like the German Empire. Instead, the war was being fought for treasures that could be stolen from a defeated nation—a way to profit from the millions of lives that had already been lost around the world.

President Wilson was outraged as well. He felt that if the Allies were intent on stealing from Germany after its defeat, peace could not be realized. When nations fought for profit instead of ideals, Wilson believed, there could be no peace, only more war.

Wilson was determined to establish his own guidelines for a fair and lasting peace. He drafted a list of conditions called the Fourteen Points, and he presented them to a joint session of Congress on January 8, 1918. In his address, Wilson said that the world was looking to the United States to negotiate international peace. He then outlined his Fourteen Points, which included the following general guidelines:

- *No secret negotiations between nations*
- *Freedom of navigation upon the seas*
- *Removal of trade barriers between countries*
- *Reduction of military weapons*

The list also included more specific guidelines concerning particular territories, nations, and governments. The last point called for the formation of an association of nations that would guarantee political independence for nations throughout the world.

At the end of his speech, Wilson appealed to Germany to stop fighting and to agree to the terms he had just outlined. "For such arrangements and covenants we are willing to fight and to continue to fight until they are achieved," he said. "We do not wish to fight her [Germany] if she is

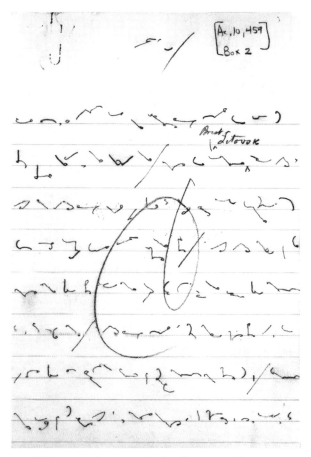

*Wilson made notes for his Fourteen Points
speech in shorthand.*

──────── ◇ ────────

willing to associate herself with us and the other peace-loving nations of the world in covenants of justice and fair dealing. We wish her only to accept a place of equality among the peoples of the world—the new world in which we now live—instead of a place of mastery." As the speech came to a close, Congress thundered with applause.

Woodrow Wilson's Fourteen Points

I. Open covenants of peace, openly arrived at, after which there shall be no private international understandings of any kind but diplomacy shall proceed always frankly and in the public view.

II. Absolute freedom of navigation upon the seas, outside territorial waters, alike in peace and in war, except as the seas may be closed in whole or in part by international action for the enforcement of international covenants.

III. The removal, so far as possible, of all economic barriers and the establishment of an equality of trade conditions among all the nations consenting to the peace and associating themselves for its maintenance.

IV. Adequate guarantees given and taken that national armaments will be reduced to the lowest point consistent with domestic safety.

V. A free, open-minded, and absolutely impartial adjustment of all colonial claims, based upon a strict observance of the principle that in determining all such questions of sovereignty the interests of the populations concerned must have equal weight with the equitable claims of the government whose title is to be determined.

VI. The evacuation of all Russian territory and such a settlement of all questions affecting Russia as will secure the best and freest cooperation of the other nations of the world in obtaining for her an unhampered and unembarrassed opportunity for the independent determination of her own political development and national policy and assure her of a sincere welcome into the society of free nations under institutions of her own choosing; and, more than a welcome, assistance also of every kind that she may need and may herself desire. The treatment accorded Russia by her sister nations in the months to come will be the acid test of their good will, of their comprehension of her needs as distinguished from their own interests, and of their intelligent and unselfish sympathy.

VII. Belgium, the whole world will agree, must be evacuated and restored, without any attempt to limit the sovereignty which she enjoys in common with all other free nations. No other single act will serve as this will serve to restore confidence among the nations in the laws which they have themselves set and determined for the government of their relations with one another. Without this healing act the whole structure and validity of international law is forever impaired.

VIII. All French territory should be freed and the invaded portions restored, and the wrong done to France by Prussia in 1871 in the matter of Alsace-Lorraine, which has unsettled the peace of the world for nearly fifty years, should be righted, in order that peace may once more be made secure in the interest of all.

IX. A readjustment of the frontiers of Italy should be effected along clearly recognizable lines of nationality.

X. The peoples of Austria-Hungary, whose place among the nations we wish to see safeguarded and assured, should be accorded the freest opportunity to autonomous development.

XI. Rumania, Serbia, and Montenegro should be evacuated; occupied territories restored; Serbia accorded free and secure access to the sea; and the relations of the several Balkan states to one another determined by friendly counsel along historically established lines of allegiance and nationality; and international guarantees of the political and economic independence and territorial integrity of the several Balkan states should be entered into.

XII. The Turkish portion of the present Ottoman Empire should be assured a secure sovereignty, but the other nationalities which are now under Turkish rule should be assured an undoubted security of life and an absolutely unmolested opportunity of autonomous development, and the Dardanelles should be permanently opened as a free passage to the ships and commerce of all nations under international guarantees.

XIII. An independent Polish state should be erected which should include the territories inhabited by indisputably Polish populations, which should be assured a free and secure access to the sea, and whose political and economic independence and territorial integrity should be guaranteed by international covenant.

XIV. A general association of nations must be formed under specific covenants for the purpose of affording mutual guarantees of political independence and territorial integrity to great and small states alike.

VICTORY FOR THE ALLIES

The fighting in Europe continued, but the armies and battlegrounds were changed. In March, the new Russian government signed a peace treaty with Germany. The Germans no longer had to fight with Russia. Thousands of German soldiers were moved from Russia to France, where they launched massive attacks on the Allies in March, April, and May.

The Germans believed that if they could capture Paris, victory was not too far away. They were stalled, however, when American armies entered the fighting. In May, the Allies were able to stop the German advance and secure Paris. By June, American forces had pushed the Germans back from all strategic positions in France.

On July 14, the Germans launched another attack on Paris, but the Allies again repelled them. The final victory of the war came in October, when 1.2 million American soldiers fought their way across the last German line of defense, the Hindenburg Line in northern France. It was a bloody battle, and thousands of lives were lost, but the Allies were victorious.

CHAPTER 10

WAR'S END

"Any influence that the American people have over the affairs of the world is measured by their sympathy with the aspirations of free men everywhere. America does love freedom, and I believe that she loves freedom unselfishly."

—Woodrow Wilson

On October 6, 1918, a message arrived in Washington: "The German Government requests the President of the United States of America to take steps for the restoration of peace. . . . The German Government has accepted the terms laid down by President Wilson in his address of January 8, and in his subsequent addresses, as the foundation of a permanent peace of justice. In order to avoid further bloodshed, the German Government requests to bring about the immediate conclusion of a general armistice on land, on water, and in the air." Germany had acknowledged defeat. The war was over.

THE DESTRUCTION OF WORLD WAR I

- About 63 million men fought in the war.

- About 8.5 million men died in the war.

- About 21 million men were wounded in the war.

- At the Battle of the Somme, the British lost nearly 60,000 men in a single day.

- At the Battle of Verdun, more than 600,000 men were killed on both sides.

- The total cost of the war was approximately $337 billion.

*A parade of returning soldiers passes in front of
the New York City Public Library.*

⸻ ✧ ⸻

The Germans accepted an armistice, a formal agreement to stop fighting, on November 11. That day the *New York Times* reported: "Last night [in France], for the first time since August in the first year of the war, there was no light of gunfire in the sky, no sudden stabs of flame through darkness, no spreading glow above black trees where for four years of nights human beings were smashed to death. The Fires of Hell had been put out."

But the British and French were upset that the Germans had sent their message directly to Woodrow Wilson, boldly ignoring the other Allied nations. The Germans had done so for a good reason: Having read Wilson's Fourteen Points, they were convinced that the United States would treat them fairly. They also knew that the other Allied leaders were not as idealistic as Wilson. They wanted to punish Germany. They wanted reparations, or payment, for the damage Germany had inflicted during the war.

PEACE TALKS IN PARIS

Allied leaders planned to meet in Paris to draw up an official peace settlement to present to Germany. President Wilson was afraid that without his presence at the meetings, the other Allied powers would ignore the Fourteen Points. So he sailed for Europe on December 4, 1918.

Peace talks began in January, with Wilson joined by Georges Clemenceau of France, David Lloyd George of Britain, and Vittorio Orlando of Italy, which had joined the Allies in 1915. Together, these men were called the Big Four.

At the meetings, Wilson talked about his Fourteen Points, explaining that the last point was the most important. He wanted to set up an international association that would help keep peace in the world and solve disputes between governments. This organization, he said, would help ensure that another major war would never take place. Wilson called this association the League of Nations. On January 25, the peace conference accepted the principle of the League of Nations and agreed to include it in the peace treaty.

The Big Four also considered Germany's future in discussions that lasted for almost four months. Wilson did not remain in Europe for the entire conference. He sailed home on February 15 and returned to Paris again on March 14. During the negotiations, Wilson had to compromise on many major issues. When the peace treaty, called the Treaty of Versailles, was finally signed on June 28, 1919, the League of Nations idea was included. But many of Wilson's other Fourteen Points were not.

In fact, the final terms for peace were very harsh for Germany. It was forced to take responsibility for causing the war. It had to hand over large amounts of territory, weapons, ships, and other goods to the Allies. It had to pay the Allies billions of dollars in reparations.

———————————— ✧ ————————————

French premier Georges Clemenceau (standing) *addresses those assembled for the signing of the Treaty of Versailles. Wilson is seated to Clemenceau's right.*

The German government and its citizens were angry over the terms of the treaty. They hadn't expected such harsh treatment, and they were furious about being blamed entirely for the war. Germany was also disappointed in the United States, particularly Woodrow Wilson. His Fourteen Points had promised Germany fair treatment, but in the end, the Germans felt, he was as dishonorable as the rest of the Allied leaders.

In actuality, Wilson was almost as disappointed with the peace treaty as Germany was. He had fought long and hard for fair terms for the Germans, but the other Allied leaders would not agree with him. He realized at one point in the negotiations that he would have to compromise or there would be no peace treaty at all.

A TURN FOR THE WORSE

Wilson sailed home on June 29, 1919, the day after the treaty was signed. On July 10 he delivered an address to the Senate, outlining the treaty and asking the senators to approve it. Most of the senators supported the agreement. But one group of Republicans opposed it. They argued against participation in the League of Nations, saying that the United States should stay out of European affairs.

Wilson was devastated but not defeated. He decided to take a tour of the country to rally support from the people. On September 3, 1919, the Wilsons boarded a train. They traveled west, stopping in cities large and small, where Wilson met with citizens and explained the terms of the treaty with Germany. In all, the couple traveled about eight thousand miles through seventeen states.

Wilson gave more than twenty speeches in twenty-two days.

But he was very tired. His term of office had been filled with major issues, both domestic and foreign. The war had taxed his strength, and he was now almost sixty-three years old. Finally, on the way to Wichita, Kansas, Wilson was

Undaunted by Senate opposition to U.S. participation in the League of Nations, Wilson (in top hat) appealed directly to the American people on a train trip through seventeen states.

taken ill. His doctor insisted that he end his tour and return immediately to Washington.

About a week later, Wilson suffered a massive stroke. He was paralyzed on his left side. He was mostly confined to bed, unable to attend meetings or make speeches, but he did continue to communicate his opinions and beliefs through writing. For the next year and a half, Congress, the cabinet, and other politicians carried on much of the government's work without Wilson's involvement. Edith Wilson also played an important role behind the scenes. She screened the president's visitors and read his papers. She decided which matters needed his attention. Many historians think that she made some decisions on Wilson's behalf during his illness—although the extent of her involvement in government affairs is not fully known.

Although in poor health, former president Wilson sometimes enjoyed going out to a play or a movie with his wife Edith.

CHAPTER ELEVEN

THE FUTURE
IS IN OUR HANDS

*"Better a thousand times to go down
fighting than to dip your colours to
dishonourable compromise."*
—Woodrow Wilson

The League of Nations was established in January 1920, but the United States was not among its members. The Senate was split over whether the United States should join, and in the end it never did. President Wilson was terribly disappointed. He believed that if the United States was not included in the league, it would not last.

Wilson's spirits were temporarily lifted when he learned that he had won the Nobel Peace Prize for his part in helping establish the League of Nations. By then, December 1920, he was too ill to travel and could not accept the prize in person. At the awards ceremony in Oslo, Norway, Albert G. Schmedeman, the American minister to Norway, read Wilson's acceptance speech on his behalf: "In accepting the honor of your award, I am moved by the recognition of my sincere and earnest efforts in the cause of peace, but also by a very poignant humility before the vastness of the work still called for by this cause....I am convinced that our generation has, despite its wounds, made notable progress, but it is the better part of wisdom to consider our work as only begun....Whatever has been accomplished in the past is petty compared to the glory of the promise of the future."

RETIREMENT AND A NEW HOME

Wilson's second term as president ended on March 4, 1921, at noon. The Wilsons decided to stay in Washington, moving into a house in a neighborhood called Embassy Row. The house was both comfortable and elegant. It had a sunroom overlooking a garden and servants' quarters in the basement. Edith arranged to have an elevator installed so that Wilson could move easily between floors. Crowds of well-wishers often passed the house and saluted him through open windows.

Edith cared for Wilson at home and read him detective stories daily. When he tired of them, she read him the works of Dickens and Scott—his favorites from childhood. Occasionally, they went to the theater or the movies and entertained friends at home. Wilson also wrote an article called "The Road Away from Revolution," an argument for a peaceful, caring, and civilized society. It was published in the *Atlantic Monthly.*

During his presidency, Wilson had established November 11, the day that fighting ended in Europe, as a holiday called Armistice Day (later called Veterans Day). On that day in 1923, a crowd assembled outside the Wilson home. Edith helped Wilson out onto the grassy lawn, where he gave his last public speech: "The future is in our hands and if we are not equal to it, the shame will be ours and none other. I thank you from a very full heart, my friends, for this demonstration of kindness by you and bid you and the nation Godspeed."

———————— ✧ ————————

Wilson (in the top hat) addresses the Armistice Day crowd from the porch of his home on Embassy Row in Washington, D.C.

HOW SUCCESSFUL WAS THE LEAGUE OF NATIONS?

To establish the League of Nations, Paris Peace Conference participants adopted a covenant, or agreement, on April 28, 1919. It began: "The high contracting parties, in order to promote international cooperation and to secure international peace and security by the acceptance of obligations not to resort to war, by the prescription of open, just and honorable relations between nations, by the firm establishment of the understandings of international law as the actual role of conduct among Governments, and by the maintenance of justice and a scrupulous respect for all treaty obligations in the dealings of organized peoples with one another, agree to this covenant of the League of Nations."

A total of sixty-three countries eventually joined the league. The United States was not among them. Unfortunately, the league was not very successful in preventing war and arbitrating disputes between nations. The world faced many crises in the years that the league operated. Several large nations invaded weaker ones, and the league was powerless to stop them.

In 1939 when fighting broke out in Europe, it became evident that Woodrow Wilson's dream of preventing another world war had not been realized. The league stopped functioning in 1939 and was formally disbanded in 1946. Many historians believe that the failure of the United States to join the league may have contributed to its downfall.

The United Nations began in 1945 to act as the league's successor. It is based on the same principles as the league: to discourage warfare, to arbitrate disputes between nations, to encourage disarmament, and to encourage diplomacy between nations.

FINAL DAYS

Woodrow Wilson suffered another stroke on January 16, 1924. Everyone close to him knew that the end was near. He died on February 3, 1924, at 11:15 in the morning. Two days later, his body was carried to Bethlehem Chapel at the Washington Cathedral. Thousands upon thousands of people lined the roads following the funeral procession.

The country deeply mourned Wilson's passing. Thousands of people sent condolence letters to his wife and daughters, and poets from all over the world wrote verses honoring his life and death. Although Wilson had brought the United States into war, the nation still looked upon him as the "president of peace."

Woodrow Wilson's ideals lived on long after he was gone—in the form of the League of Nations and later the United Nations. Even those who had opposed his policies came to appreciate his heartfelt spirit, his courage in the face of trouble, and his faith in the American people. Many have called him one of the finest presidents who ever sat in the White House, not just because he was a great political leader but also because he was, first and foremost, a great human being.

TIMELINE

1856 Thomas Woodrow Wilson is born on December 28 in Staunton, Virginia. His parents are Janet and Joseph Wilson. He has two older sisters and later a younger brother. He is called Tommy as a boy.

1857 The Wilson family moves to Augusta, Georgia. This move puts them in the heart of the South during the Civil War.

1861 The Civil War begins when Tommy is four years old. The Wilsons and other people in Augusta face hunger and hardship during the war.

1870 When Tommy is thirteen years old, the Wilsons move to Columbia, South Carolina. Dr. Wilson takes a teaching job at a seminary there.

1873 Sixteen-year-old Thomas Wilson, now introducing himself as Woodrow Wilson, enters Davidson College. His father hopes he will become a minister.

1874 Wilson becomes ill and returns home from college. He spends his time reading, taking walks, and practicing his speaking skills.

1875 Wilson enters Princeton University. There, he decides that he wants to become an orator and a statesman.

1879 Wilson graduates from Princeton, thirty-eighth in his class. His father is disappointed with his ranking. Wilson enrolls at the University of Virginia Law School. He feels that a legal career will lead him into politics.

1882 Wilson passes his exams and becomes a lawyer. He moves to Atlanta, Georgia, and opens a law firm with a friend.

1883 While handling some business for his mother in Georgia, Wilson meets Ellen Louise Axson. Disillusioned with the practice of law, Wilson enrolls in Johns Hopkins University. He begins graduate work in political science.

1885 Wilson accepts a teaching position at Bryn Mawr College in Philadelphia, an all-women's school. He marries Ellen Louise Axson.

1886 Ellen gives birth to their first daughter, Margaret.

1887 A second daughter, Jessie Woodrow, is born. Wilson worries about making enough money to support his growing family.

1888 Wilson joins the faculty of Wesleyan University. The family moves to Connecticut.

1889 A third daughter, Eleanor Randolph, is born.

1890 Wilson becomes a professor at Princeton University.

1902 Wilson becomes president of Princeton University. This position marks the end of his career as a scholar.

1910 Wilson resigns as president of Princeton to campaign for governor of New Jersey. He wins the election by a large majority.

1912 The Democratic Party nominates Wilson for president of the United States. He runs against William Howard Taft and Theodore Roosevelt. Wilson wins the election.

1913 Wilson signs the Federal Reserve Act, strengthening the nation's banking system.

1914 World War I breaks out in Europe. Wilson promises that the United States will remain neutral in the conflict. Ellen Wilson dies of Bright's disease.

1915 Germany sinks a British passenger ship, the *Lusitania,* with more than one hundred American citizens aboard. Support for neutrality weakens. Wilson marries Edith Bolling Galt.

1916 Wilson is nominated for president a second time. Preoccupied with the war in Europe, he does very little campaigning but still wins the election.

1917 British agents intercept the Zimmermann note. The United States declares war on Germany. Wilson signs the Selective Draft Act to build up U.S. military forces.

1918 Wilson outlines his Fourteen Points for peace at a joint session of Congress. His plan includes creation of the League of Nations to serve as a future peacekeeping body. World War I ends. Wilson goes to Paris to represent the United States at a peace conference.

1919 The Treaty of Versailles is signed in Paris. Wilson tours the United States, trying to rally support for the League of Nations. He suffers a massive stroke and returns to Washington for medical attention.

1920 Wilson wins the prestigious Nobel Peace Prize. He is too ill to travel to Norway for the award ceremony.

1921 Wilson's second term as president ends. He and Edith move to a house in Washington, D.C.

1923 Wilson speaks to a crowd gathered in front of his home on Armistice Day. It is his last public speech.

1924 Woodrow Wilson dies at 11:15 A.M. on February 3.

SOURCE NOTES

7   John Randolph Bolling,
    *Chronology of Woodrow
    Wilson* (New York: Frederick
    A. Stokes Company, 1927),
    78.
8   Ibid., 218–230.
9   Ibid.
10 Alfred S. Steinberg, *Woodrow
    Wilson* (New York: G. P.
    Putnam's Sons, 1961), 18.
12–13 Sigmund Freud and William
    Bullitt, *Thomas Woodrow
    Wilson: A Psychological Study*
    Boston: Houghton Mifflin
    Company, 1967), 10.
18 Steinberg, 24.
23 Ibid., 30.
25 Ibid., 35.
30 John A. Garraty, *Woodrow
    Wilson: A Great Life in Brief*
    (New York: Alfred A. Knopf,
    1956), 9.
30 Steinberg, 43.
30 Garraty, 10.
31 Ibid., 17.
33 Ibid., 13.
35 Alden Hatch, *Edith Bolling
    Wilson: First Lady
    Extraordinary* (New York:
    Dodd, Mead & Co., 1961),
    56.
36–37 Garraty, 16.
39 Ibid., 25.
40 Frances Wright Saunders,
    *First Lady between Two
    Worlds: Ellen Axson Wilson*
    (Chapel Hill, NC: University
    of North Carolina Press,
    1985), 119.
40-41 Garraty, 17.
41 Ibid., 20.
45 August Heckscher, *Woodrow
    Wilson: A Biography* (New
    York: Charles Scribner's Sons,
    1991), 201.
47 Ibid., 218.
49 Saunders, 212.

49–50 Ibid., 216.
54 Garraty, 68.
55 Saunders, 221.
57 Josephus Daniels, *The Life of
    Woodrow Wilson, 1856-1924*
    (Chicago: John C. Winston
    Co., 1924), 329.
61 Garraty, 33.
62 Saunders, 247.
62–63 Ibid., 251.
65 Ibid., 276.
66 Garraty, 98.
68 Bolling, 190–192.
70 Ibid., 76–77.
75 Ibid., 231.
76 Ibid.
76 Ibid.
76 Ibid., 233.
78–79 Ibid., 98.
82–83 Ibid., 258–259.
88 Ibid., 272.
88 Ibid., 114.
90 *World War I Document
    Archives*, February 5, 1996,
    <http://www.lib.byu.edu/~rdh
    /ww1/1918/nytend.html>.
97 Garraty, 186.
98 Bolling, 162–163.
99 Ibid., 166.
100 Ibid., 366.

BIBLIOGRAPHY

Axson, Stockton. *Brother Woodrow: A Memoir of Woodrow Wilson.* Princeton, NJ: Princeton University Press, 1993.

Baker, Ray Stannard. *Woodrow Wilson: Life and Letters: Youth 1856–1890.* New York: Doubleday, Page & Co., 1927.

Bolling, John Randolph. *Chronology of Woodrow Wilson.* New York: Frederick A. Stokes Company, 1927.

Bragdon, Henry Wilkinson. *Woodrow Wilson: The Academic Years.* Cambridge, MA: Belkamp Press of Harvard University Press, 1967.

Daniels, Josephus. *The Life of Woodrow Wilson, 1856–1924.* Chicago: John C. Winston Co., 1924.

————. *The Wilson Era: Years of Peace—1910–1917.* Chapel Hill, NC: University of North Carolina Press, 1944.

Day, Donald, ed. *Woodrow Wilson's Own Story.* Boston: Little, Brown & Co., 1952.

Freud, Sigmund, and William Bullitt. *Thomas Woodrow Wilson: A Psychological Study.* Boston: Houghton Mifflin Company, 1967.

Fussell, Paul. *The Great War and Modern Memory.* New York: Oxford University Press, 1975.

Garraty, John A. *Woodrow Wilson: A Great Life in Brief.* New York: Alfred A. Knopf, 1956.

Gilbert, Martin. *First World War.* London: Weidenfeld and Nicolson, 1994.

Hatch, Alden. *Edith Bolling Wilson: First Lady Extraordinary.* New York: Dodd, Mead & Co., 1961.

————. *Woodrow Wilson.* New York: Holt, Rinehart and Winston, 1947.

Heckscher, August. *Woodrow Wilson: A Biography.* New York: Charles Scribner's Sons, 1991.

Keegan, John. *The First World War.* New York: Alfred A. Knopf, 1999.

McAdoo, Eleanor Wilson. *The Woodrow Wilsons.* New York: Macmillan Company, 1937.

Mulder, John M. *Woodrow Wilson: The Years of Preparation.* Princeton, NJ: Princeton University Press, 1978.

Saunders, Frances Wright. *First Lady between Two Worlds: Ellen Axson Wilson.* Chapel Hill, NC: University of North Carolina Press, 1985.

Seldes, George. *Witness to a Century.* New York: Ballantine Books, 1987.

Shachtman, Tom. *Edith and Woodrow: A Presidential Romance.* New York: G. P. Putnam's Sons, 1981.

Smith, Gene. *When the Cheering Stopped: The Last Years of Woodrow Wilson.* New York: William Morrow and Company, 1964.

Steinberg, Alfred S. *Woodrow Wilson.* New York: G. P. Putnam's Sons, 1961.

Taylor, A. J. P. *The First World War.* London: Penguin Books, 1966.

Vansittart, Peter. *Voices from the Great War.* London: Penguin Books, 1983.

FURTHER READING

Allan, Tony. *The Causes of World War I*. Chicago: Heinemann Library, 2002.

American Experience: Woodrow Wilson
<http://www.pbs.org/wgbh/amex/wilson/>

Brittain, Vera. *Testament of Youth: An Autobiographical Study of the Years 1900–1925*. 1933. Reprint, New York: Penguin, 1994.

Collier, Christopher, and James Lincoln Collier. *The U.S. Enters the World Stage: 1867–1919*. New York: Benchmark Books, 2000.

Currie, Stephen. *Life in the Trenches*. Farmington Hills, MI: Gale Group, 2001.

Damon, Duane. *Growing Up in the Civil War*. Minneapolis: Lerner Publications Company, 2003.

Dolan, Edward. *America in World War I*. Brookfield, CT: Millbrook Press, 1996.

"Edith Bolling Galt Wilson." *The White House*.
<http://www.whitehouse.gov/history/firstladies/ew28-2.html>

"Ellen Louise Axson Wilson." *The White House*.
<http://www.whitehouse.gov/history/firstladies/ew28-1.html>

Feinstein, Stephen. *The 1910s: From World War I to Ragtime Music*. Berkeley Heights, NJ: Enslow Publishers, 2001.

Flanagan, Alice K. *Edith Bolling Galt Wilson*. Danbury, CT: Children's Press, 1999.

Hudson, Edward, comp. *Poetry of the First World War*. East Sussex, England: Wayland Publishers Ltd., 1988.

Kent, Zachary. *World War I: The War to End Wars*. Berkeley Heights, NJ: Enslow Publishers, 1994.

McPhail, Helen, and Philip Guest. *Wilfred Owen: On the Trail of the Poets of the Great War*. London: Leo Cooper, 1999.

Randolph, Sallie G. *Woodrow Wilson, President*. New York: Walker & Company, 1992.

Remarque, Erich Maria. *All Quiet on the Western Front*. 1929. Reprint, New York: Fawcett Books, 1995.

Schraff, Anne. *Woodrow Wilson*. Berkelcy Heights, NJ: Enslow Publishers, 1998.

Stone, Tanya Lee. *The Progressive Era and World War I*. Austin, TX: Raintree/Steck Vaughn, 2001.

Taylor, David. *Key Battles of World War I*. Chicago: Heinemann Library, 2002.

Tuchman, Barbara W. *The Zimmermann Telegram*. 1958. Reprint, New York: Ballantine Books, 1985.

Uschan, Michael. *The 1910s*. San Diego: Lucent Books, 1999.

"Wars & Conflict: World War One." *BBC History*. <http://www.bbc.co.uk/history/war/wwone/index.shtml>

Woodrow Wilson House <http://www.woodrowwilsonhouse.org/>

INDEX

ABOUT THE AUTHOR

Carol Dommermuth-Costa has worked in the classroom as a teacher and in publishing as an editor. She works as a freelance writer and artist. Ms. Dommermuth-Costa has also written *Nikola Tesla: A Spark of Genius, Agatha Christie: Writer of Mystery, Emily Dickinson: Singular Poet, Indira Gandhi: Daughter of India,* and *William Shakespeare.* She lives in Mamaroneck, New York.
